HOW UNIVERSE?

NIHAL MUDGAL

DEDICATED TO YOU...

May the universe bring you love and joy for your entire existence.

That is my intention for you

and for the world.

Contents

GRATITUDE   *vii*

Acknowledgements   *ix*

Preface   *xi*

Foreword   *xiii*

INTRODUCTION   *xvii*

1. UNDERSTANDING THE UNIVERSE   1

2. THE SCIENCE OF MANIFESTATION   7

3. LETTING GO FEAR AND DOUBTS   14

4. SPIRITUAL GROWTH AND PRACTICES   21

5. APPLYING UNIVERSE LAWS   34

6. RISE ABOVE CHALLENGES FROM THE UNIVERSE   40

7. UNVEILING THE MYSTERY OF UNIVERSE   48

8. TRUST THE UNIVERSE   56

9. UNIVERSE SECRET REVEALED   63

ABOUT THE AUTHOR   69

MESSAGE FROM THE AUTHOR   71

Gratitude

To my beloved '**Lord Shri Hari**',

I offer my deepest, most heartfelt gratitude to You, the Divine Source of all creation, wisdom, and inspiration. Your loving guidance and presence have been the driving force behind the creation of this book, "HOW UNIVERSE?".

Your divine hand has gently led me through the journey of writing this book, illuminating my path with the light of knowledge, wisdom, and understanding. Your love and grace have filled my heart with the desire to share the secrets of the universe with humanity, and to inspire others to connect with Your divine presence.

I am but a humble instrument of Your will, and I acknowledge that every word, every sentence, and every page of this book is a manifestation of Your divine inspiration. I am grateful for the opportunity to serve as a vessel for Your message, and I pray that it may touch the hearts and minds of all who read it.

May this book be a testament to Your love, wisdom, and power, and may it inspire others to seek a deeper connection with You. I offer my heartfelt thanks to You, dear Lord Shri Hari, for Your guidance, love, and inspiration.

Shri Hari!

Acknowledgements

As I bring this book to life, I am filled with gratitude for the countless individuals who have supported me on this journey.

To my loved ones, who have endured countless hours of my absence, distraction, and enthusiastic sharing of spiritual concepts – thank you for your unwavering love, patience, and encouragement.

To My beloved **LORD SHRI HARI**, My guru SHRI ANIRUDHACHARYA JI, SHRI PREMANAND JI MAHARAJ, My teacher SHREYAS MUKATI SIR, My Parents GAGAN MUDGAL & ANJALI MUDGAL, who have shared their wisdom, insights, and experiences with me – I am forever grateful for the lessons you have taught me and the paths you have illuminated.

To the readers of my first book, **"Why Universe?"**, whose feedback, questions, and testimonials inspired me to write this sequel – thank you for your engagement, curiosity, and enthusiasm.

And to the **UNIVERSE** itself, which has been my greatest teacher, guide, and source of inspiration – I offer my deepest gratitude for the mysteries you have revealed to me, the lessons you have taught me, and the love you have shared with me.

This book is a testament to the power of collaboration, community, and the universal spirit that connects us all. Thank you to everyone who has contributed to its creation.

With love and appreciation,

NIHAL MUDGAL

SHRI RADHA!

Preface

As I sit in stillness, reflecting on the journey that has led me to write these words, I am reminded of the profound wisdom that lies within and around us. The universe, in all its mystery and majesty, holds the secrets to unlocking our full potential, manifesting our deepest desires, and living a life of purpose and fulfillment.

My own journey of discovery, which began with the questions posed in my first book, **"WHY UNIVERSE?"**, has led me to the realization that the universe is not just a vast expanse of space and time, but a dynamic, interconnected web of energy and consciousness that responds to our thoughts, emotions, and intentions.

In **"HOW UNIVERSE?"**, I invite you to join me on a journey of exploration and discovery, as we delve into the practical wisdom and spiritual principles that govern the universe and our place within it. Through a combination of scientific insights, spiritual teachings, and personal anecdotes, we will explore the mechanisms of manifestation, the power of intention, and the art of aligning ourselves with the universe's infinite potential.

My intention in writing this book is not to provide a definitive answer to the mysteries of the universe, but to offer a guiding light on the path to discovery, and to empower you with the tools and insights necessary to unlock your full potential and live a life that reflects your deepest desires and highest aspirations.

So, come with me on this journey of exploration and discovery, and let us uncover the secrets of the universe together.

NIHAL MUDGAL

Foreword

As we navigate the complexities of our modern world, it's easy to lose sight of the profound wisdom that lies within and around us. We search for answers to life's biggest questions – Who am I? Why am I here? What is the purpose of life? – without realizing that the universe itself holds the secrets to unlocking our full potential.

In **"HOW UNIVERSE?"**, NIHAL MUDGAL offers a masterful guide to understanding the mysteries of the universe and our place within it. Building on the insights of "Why Universe?", this book provides a comprehensive roadmap for manifesting our deepest desires, cultivating spiritual growth, and connecting with the universe's infinite potential.

With clarity, compassion, and a deep understanding of the human condition, NIHAL MUDGAL shares practical wisdom, scientific insights, and personal anecdotes that will inspire, educate, and empower you. Whether you're a spiritual seeker, a curious explorer, or simply someone looking for a deeper sense of purpose and meaning, this book has the potential to transform your life.

As you embark on this journey, remember that the universe is not just a vast expanse of space and time – it's a dynamic, interconnected web of energy and consciousness that responds to our thoughts, emotions, and intentions. By applying the principles outlined in this book, you'll not only gain a deeper understanding of the universe, but also discover the power to shape your own reality.

So, come with an open heart, an inquiring mind, and a willingness to explore the mysteries of the universe. The journey ahead promises to be transformative, enlightening, and profoundly life-changing.

| Sachidanand Rupaya Vishvotpatyadi Hetave |

|| Tapatraya Vinashaya Shri Krishnaya Vayam Namaha ||

~Shrimadbhagawat Mahapuran[8TH CENTURY]

Introduction

Before we begin, I think it's worth reminding ourselves of this: **manifesting is not just about attracting 'things' into our lives or manifesting how we want our lives to appear to others. No, it is about manifesting a life that makes us feel content and fulfilled, and one that allows us to experience joy, excitement and love. Getting to the crux of what will bring you those feelings is the key.**

TO MANIFEST:

"To make something happen"

Whenever I get asked, 'What exactly is manifesting?' I say this: **'Manifesting is the ability to use the power of your mind to change and create the reality you experience. It is a self-development practice to live by.'** To me manifesting is the umbrella of self-development, and all self-help and inner healing falls beneath it. It is why I believe it can help to empower and transform the lives of each and every person that practises it.

Manifesting is not this mystical fluffy practice that some people think it is. It's not just about positive thinking or visualizing what you want. It's not about a constant pursuit of more, more, more. It's not a ritual that you do for twenty minutes a day. **Manifesting is a way of living. It is about unlocking the most powerful, magnetic and confident version of yourself that exists so that you can make things happen. It's about making the life you have feel the best that it can be. It isn't magic at all, but the results of it feel magical.**

I hope that after reading my "WHY UNIVERSE?" book, you can understand how limitless you really are, and how much power you hold within you. I hope you have started to uncover your most authentic self and begun to heal all the wounds that life has left you with. I hope that you start to really believe the truth: that you are enough, that you have always been enough and that you deserve to live a life that makes you feel excited to get out of bed each day. You are worthy of all the happiness, love, success and abundance that the universe has to offer. I really wish I could have told my younger self what I want to tell you now:

"LIFE IS WONDERFUL AND YOU HAVE THE POWER TO MAKE IT SO"

Just ask yourself : When was the last time you sat and gave yourself credit for how much you've grown and how far you've come? When was the last time you celebrated a relatively small win, just because? When was the last time you just sat down and said out loud, **"I'm really really proud of myself?"**

"CELEBRATE YOURSELF, NOBODY KNOWS WHAT IT TAKES TO BE YOU."

-NIHAL MUDGAL

ONE

UNDERSTANDING THE UNIVERSE

The seeker sat near the shore of a vast, endless Ocean, where the soft waves caressed the sands in lulling whispers. The sky overhead arched itself into infinity, its colours bleeding across the brushstrokes of galaxies that danced like pearls set in the universe's canvas, Pearlescent stars studded the heavens, casting their ghostly light onto the world, There was a gentle breeze that threaded its way through the atmosphere, bringing with it the smell of salt and intrigue, as though the world itself breathed in time with the seeker,

He shut his eyes, feeling the cool breeze brush against his body and hearing the melody of the waves. It was a night like no other a night alive, as though the universe was sharing secrets with those who would listen. In that holy instant, he sensed it: the intangible thread that bound him to all. **The expansiveness of the universe, the profundity of the sea, the beat of his own heart-all of it part of the same great plan.**

An idea came to him: **What is the universe?** Not just scientifically, but in its most basic, most essential form. **Is it a cluster of stars, planets, and cosmic debris? Or is it something else a thinking force, a great consciousness, an endless playground of possibility?**

The seeker had wandered for years, searching for answers, drifting through the maze of ancient scriptures, scientific findings, and spiritual epiphanies. But, here, under this expansive, star-filled sky, he understood that **the universe was not something to be known by knowledge alone. It was to be felt, to be experienced.**

The universe has a language that is not of words a language of vibration, energy, and synchronicities. Every star that flickers, every ripple in the ocean, every wind that blows carries a message for those willing to listen. He remembered instances in his life when coincidences were too perfect, too coincidental to be coincidence. Was it the universe calling him? Was it some unseen force pushing him toward his fate?

Science reminds us that the universe is a field of energy. Everything from the galaxies in the sky above to the sands beneath his fingers is made up of vibrating particles. Even his thoughts, feelings, and desires had a frequency, shaping the world around him in ways undetectable. The awareness made him shudder, He was not just a spectator of the universe; he was a complex part of it, woven into its fabric.

He scooped up a smooth rock from the beach and threw it into the water. It settled with a gentle plop, and ripples radiated outward in flawless circles, rippling the reflection of the moon. The gesture was straightforward, but it was very true. Every emotion, every action, every thought sends out ripples that reach far beyond what can be seen. This was the law of cause and effect the law that energy released into the universe always returns.

The seeker breathed deep, letting the wisdom of the night settle within him. Being wise about the universe wasn't about solving every one of its mysteries; it was about joining its rhythm, accepting its flow, and accepting that he never stood apart from it. The stars, the sea, the wind they all reflected the same cosmic energy streaming through him.

He smiled, looking up at the galaxies above. At that moment, he was not merely a wanderer searching for answers. He was a co-creator of his reality, a being of light and energy, a child of the universe. And as the waves continued their eternal dance, **he knew his journey had only just begun..**

"Both faith and fear demands you to believe in something you cannot see -You choose."

"The Universe as an Intelligent Force"

To know the universe is not to learn of its stars or to quantify its enormity. It is to see its consciousness, to see its intelligence streaming through every atom of being. Science informs us that all things-our bodies, the trees, the ocean, the nebulae beyond our reach are made up of vibrating energy. The same forces that burn stars run through our veins, and the same cosmic dust that gave birth to galaxies is within us.

Throughout the ages, mystics, philosophers, and scientists have all tried to decipher the messages of the universe. The ancients looked up at the starry sphere and did not merely see points of light; they saw divine guidance, a complex tapestry of signs pointing them toward deeper truths. Modern physics also talks of this interconnectedness-the quantum entanglement that holds particles together across space, defying all logic but testifying to the universe's unseen oneness.

"The Cosmic Whispers: Signs and Synchronicities"

Did you ever have a moment that was so well timed you felt like the universe was directly communicating with you? A song that comes on when you need to hear it, a meeting that occurs unexpectedly, a vision that later manifests in reality -these are not accidents. These are the cosmic whispers of the universe calling you onto your best path.

The seeker opened their eyes and gazed out into the expanse of night. How many times had they dismissed these whispers? How many times had doubt and fear smothered the quiet voice that urged them forward? The stars, steadfast and timeless, twinkled back as if in answer, telling them that knowing the universe demanded listening-and not with ears, but with intuition.

"The Power of Thought and Emotion"

Think about it: each of your thoughts, each of your emotions, creates waves out into the universe. Like a stone cast into a pool of water, the waves radiate outward, touching everything they encounter. This is the law of cause and effect, the universal principle of energy flow.

When you emanate love, appreciation, and positivity, the universe reflects that back to you in chances, blessings, and instances of sheer alignment. When you're stuck in fear, doubt, or resentment, you build resistance, breaking the flow of abundance that is longing to find you.

"The Seeker's Realization"

The breeze brought a new whisper, a truth coming into the seeker's mind. **The universe was not outside of them; it was inside them. The fact that they were seeking answers outside was an illusion everything they were looking for was already ingrained in their very being, ready to be unlocked.**

The ocean waves went on their eternal cadence, and the galaxies up above whirled in their heavenly dance. The seeker smiled, knowing now that to learn the universe is to learn about oneself. It was not intellectually knowing; it was experiencing, feeling, and being.

"A Journey, Not a Destination"

"Understanding the universe is not a destination—it's a journey."

Learning about the universe isn't a matter of coming to a last word-it's a matter of setting out. It's a matter of embracing the mystery, of being in awe of what we don't know, and of recognizing that every instant is a chance to draw closer to the grand cosmic power that we are an integral part of.

So stand under the stars, breathe in deeply, and remind yourself: you are not little, and you are not alone. You are the universe knowing itself, and that is a force beyond computation.

"The Universe will mirror your energy back to you. The quality of your thoughts, your actions, and the words you speak impact the quality of your life. Surround yourself with people who build you up. Ask for help. Pray, Do everything you can to feel good about being alive. The Universe will respond to how you feel, in all ways, always."
-NIHAL MUDGAL

TWO
THE SCIENCE OF MANIFESTATION

At the holy silence of morning, when the sky was sharing secrets with the ground and the first golden beam touched the horizon, the Seeker stood at the Ocean's side. His eyes, lanterns kindled by desire, looked out upon the flowing waves. The ocean glimmered not only with light, but with the eternal rhythms of the universe. It was here, on the threshold of breath and quiet, that his search into the science of manifestation fully commenced.

The Seeker had always felt that there was something more to life than chance. He could feel the draw of something greater, a higher intelligence threading its way through all things. His spirit longed for answers not only in scripture or science, but in where they met — where energy took on matter, thoughts created reality, and intention could warp the very fabric of reality.

"The Invisible Blueprint"

As he sat in contemplation, a voice within him awakened: **"The universe is not responding to you; it is reacting to you."**

That one sentence broke open a new level of perception. What if reality wasn't something that was done to him, but something he co-created? He remembered the lessons of mystics and scientists both — of how all things in existence hummed with frequency. That his thoughts, feelings, and intentions sent out vibrations. And those vibrations had energy.

In this instant, **the Seeker knew that manifestation was not simply wishfulness or mystical fantasy. It was a sacred science, governed by principles older than gravity itself.**

"Energy: The Pulse of the Universe"

Every thought, every emotion, every belief that we hold is energy. The Seeker discovered the work of Nikola Tesla, who said, "If you want to find the secrets of the universe, think in terms of energy, frequency, and vibration."

He started playing around with awareness. When he concentrated on thankfulness, he felt how light his body was, how synchronicities manifested. When fear or uncertainty filled his mind, the world felt slow, blocked, or random.

It hit him: manifestation isn't about making a wish and waiting for it to materialize; it is about becoming a vibrational match to what you want.

"You don't attract what you desire; you attract what you become."

"Quantum Field: The Playground of Possibilities"

Along the way, the Seeker learned about the quantum field — **a space where all possible realities coexist.** Quantum physicists had long referred to the **"observer effect"**: that particles exist in a state of probability until they are observed, then collapse into a definite outcome.

This flabbergasted him. **If particles were affected by observation, then consciousness shaped matter.** He knew now why intention, belief, and feeling were so important. His thoughts weren't mind chatter; they were commands emitted into the field of limitless possibility.

Reality, therefore, wasn't set. It was malleable. And **the mind was the sculptor**

"Neuroplasticity: Rewiring the Self"

Science aided this shift, not only spiritually but biologically. The Seeker discovered the concept of **neuroplasticity — the brain's capacity to rewire itself in response to new thoughts, behaviors, and experiences.**

He started to transform his inner reality. He would imagine his dreams with feeling. Not only imagining them in his mind, but feeling them in his heart. With each repetition, each affirmation, each meditation, he was reprogramming his brain to believe a new narrative.

And **when belief and feeling were in sync, and feeling and thought were in sync, miracles happened.**

"The Ripple Effect"

As you come to understand and excel in the art of manifestation, something amazing occurs. Your energy changes, and the world around you adjusts. You draw people, circumstances, and experiences that align with your new vibration. This ripple effect goes beyond you, inspiring other people to tap into their own ability to create.

The manifestation science is both easy and deep. **It's a Dance among your actions, thoughts, and the universe's infinite intelligence.** <u>By trusting the process, believing in your dreams, and aligning your energy, you have the power to change your life-and, by doing so, change the world.</u>

"The Role of Emotion"

Emotion, he came to understand, was the universe's language. Not cold logic, but fiery feeling. The universe heard not the words, but the vibration underneath them.

If he prayed for abundance in fear, he was sending lack. If he wanted love but felt inadequate, he was sending resistance. The secret was to feel now what he wanted to feel later.

Joy, appreciation, love, and wonder became his guide. They lifted his vibration. And from this higher place, manifestation became second nature.

"The Mirror Principle"

Reality started to mirror his inner changes. **The Seeker observed the external reality not as reality but as a mirror. Individuals, situations, even "accidents" were feedback loops, reflecting to him where his vibration lay.**

When he faced challenges, he no longer said, "Why is this happening to me?" Instead, he said, "What is this revealing to me about myself?"

He no longer struggled with the mirror. He transformed the image within.

"Gratitude as a Catalyst"

Every morning, the Seeker listed things he was thankful for — not begrudgingly, but reverence. Gratitude, he discovered, opened doors. It attuned him to the vibration of abundance.

Gratitude spoke to the universe: **"I trust you."And trust engaged flow.**

"Healing the Past, Opening the Future"

Old wounds rose up. **Childhood doubts. Past failures that had once defined him. He did not flee from them. He met them with compassion. He rewrote those stories not with denial, but with love.**

He understood: to create a new future, he needed to let go of the energetic burden of the past. Forgiveness was not weakness. It was freedom.

"Inspired Action: The Missing Piece"

Manifestation was not passive. It was interactive. The Seeker made inspired moves — not out of fear, but alignment. When the inner voice nudged, he moved. When doors opened, he walked through.

Faith without works, he realized, was fantasy. But belief followed by aligned action was co-creation.

"The Sacred Pause"

There were seasons of silence. Of waiting. Of uncertainty.

But even those were part of the process. **The earth lies dormant before it flowers. The womb is dark before it gives birth.**

He learned to respect the pause. To believe in the unseen. To understand that just because he couldn't see it, didn't mean it wasn't happening.

"Living as If"

The Seeker started living as if his dreams were already true. He walked with assurance, talked with enthusiasm, acted with intention.

He became the version of himself that had already received.

And the universe, as he became that version, shifted to accommodate.

"Synchronicity: The Universe Speaks"

Signs were his friends — repeating numbers, feathers along the way, strangers telling him exactly what he needed to hear. These weren't accidents. They were affirmations.

Synchronicities were the universe's "You're on track. Keep moving."

"The Unified Field of Consciousness"

Finally, the Seeker transcended the individual and reached the universal. He sensed himself not as a seperate self, but as of the One Mind, the One Heart.

He understood that what he requested wasn't solely for him. His wishes, when pure, were God's impulses wanting expression through him.

He no longer manifested out of ego, but from soul.

"Service and Surrender"

And when his expressions came -- the love, the health, the opportunities -- he did not grasp. He returned them in service.

For real manifestation, he came to know, is not about holding on. It is about expression.

And through that expression, the Seeker learned the highest truth:

That manifestation is not the science of holding, but the art of remembering.

Remembering that we are creators.

Remembering that we are energy.

Remembering that the universe lives not above us or around us, but within us.

And as the Ocean flowed beside him, reflecting the sun, the Seeker smiled, For he no longer chased the current.

He had become it......

"The stress you feel won't last. Your anxiety is only a temporary thing. It's hard to believe but it's a fact. It may take a while, but better days will come to you & when they do, embrace them without doubt. You deserve them. Soon you will feel alive again. Stay strong."

Be calm. -***NIHAL MUDGAL***

THREE

LETTING GO
FEAR AND
DOUBTS

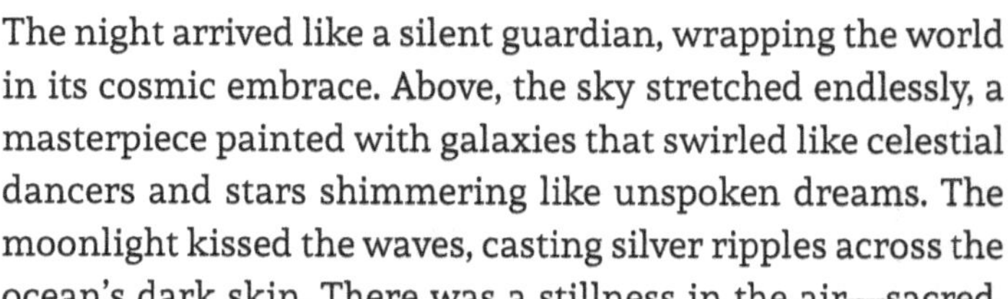

The night arrived like a silent guardian, wrapping the world in its cosmic embrace. Above, the sky stretched endlessly, a masterpiece painted with galaxies that swirled like celestial dancers and stars shimmering like unspoken dreams. The moonlight kissed the waves, casting silver ripples across the ocean's dark skin. There was a stillness in the air—sacred, calming, eternal.

The seeker sat on a rock near the shoreline, their eyes lost in the infinite expanse above. The salty breeze carried more than just the scent of the sea—it carried whispers, messages from the Universe. It wasn't the sound of the waves or the distant cries of seabirds. It was something deeper, something wordless yet profound.

Through their journey, the seeker had discovered that manifestation was more than just thoughts—it was a frequency, a vibration that shaped reality. Science had confirmed what ancient wisdom had long known—beliefs influence neurochemistry, intention rewires the brain, and the Universe, like a cosmic mirror, reflects the energy we project into it.

Yet, a deeper lesson was now unfolding—one that no amount of visualizations or techniques could bypass.

Letting go....

More specifically, **letting go of fear and doubt.**

A familiar weight pressed against the seeker's chest—not physical, but emotional. It was as if an unseen force had wrapped itself around their heart. As their gaze followed the constellation-strewn sky, a silent question arose: **"Why do I still feel fear and uncertainty, even when I believe?"**

And as if the night itself responded, a memory surfaced...

"The Garden of Fear"

As a child, the seeker had once stood in a garden, clutching a paper kite, eager to release it into the sky. The wind was playful, the sun warm, and their heart filled with joy. But each time the kite lifted, a voice called out from behind, "Be careful! Don't let it go too high—you'll lose control."

Those words, repeated over the years, became seeds of doubt, taking root in their subconscious. It wasn't just about kites—it was about dreams, ambitions, love, and trust. Every desire became entangled with a hesitant **"what if?"** *What if it doesn't work? What if I'm not enough? What if the Universe doesn't respond?*

Fear begins this way—quietly, innocently—masquerading as caution, protection, even wisdom. **Over time, it weaves itself into our beliefs, shaping every decision, every action, every unspoken hesitation.**

"The Psychology of Fear and Doubt"

Fear and doubt are not just fleeting emotions; they are deeply wired into the human psyche. At their core, **they are survival mechanisms, designed to protect us from harm. But in the modern world, these mechanisms often work against us rather than for us.**

"Fear: The Brain's Alarm System"

Fear is primarily governed by the **amygdala**, a small almond-shaped structure deep within the brain. This region is responsible for detecting threats and triggering the body's fight-or-flight response. In prehistoric times, this response was crucial for survival—helping early humans escape predators, avoid danger, and stay alive.

However, in today's world, the threats we face are rarely physical. Instead of lions or wild animals, **we fear failure, rejection, judgment, and uncertainty**. Our brain does not distinguish between real and perceived danger, so it reacts the same way to an upcoming job interview, a new relationship, or a leap of faith as it would to an actual life-threatening situation. The heart races, palms sweat, and our body prepares for battle—even though there is no physical danger present.

When fear becomes chronic, it hijacks the nervous system, keeping us in a perpetual state of hyper-vigilance. This not only affects our ability to manifest but also impacts mental and physical health, leading to **anxiety, stress, and even illness.**

"Doubt: The Voice of Past Wounds"

While fear is a reaction to perceived danger, doubt is a learned response shaped by past experiences. *Doubt arises when we have encountered failure, rejection, or disappointment repeatedly, programming our subconscious mind to expect the worst.*

Doubt is reinforced by societal conditioning as well. From an early age, many of us are told to "be realistic," "not aim too high," or "prepare for the worst." While these statements are meant to instill caution, they often plant limiting beliefs that undermine confidence and faith. Over time, doubt becomes an internal voice that whispers:

"What if I fail?"

"I'm not good enough."

"I don't deserve success."

"Things never work out for me."

These beliefs create self-fulfilling prophecies, shaping reality through a negative feedback loop. If we doubt our ability to succeed, we hesitate to take action. If we hesitate, we miss opportunities. If we miss opportunities, we reinforce the belief that success is out of reach.

"Fear, Doubt, and Manifestation"

Fear and doubt are powerful energetic blocks in the manifestation process. Manifestation is based on vibrational alignment—meaning that **what we experience externally mirrors what we believe internally.** The Universe responds not just to what we want, but to the dominant energy we emit.

If our dominant energy is one of fear or doubt, it sends mixed signals. Imagine wanting abundance but fearing financial instability. The fear creates a contradiction in your vibration, making it difficult for abundance to flow. The same applies to love, health, and success—when we desire something but secretly doubt our worthiness or fear loss, we create an energetic resistance.

This is why some manifestations seem delayed or blocked. It is not that the Universe is withholding what we desire, but that our energy is not fully aligned with receiving it. **To truly manifest, we must first clear the internal blocks of fear and doubt, shifting our vibration to one of certainty and trust.**

"Spiritual Surrender vs. Emotional Resistance"

The seeker closed their eyes, letting the ocean's rhythm speak to them. Each wave whispered a truth that could only be felt, not taught.

Manifestation is not about control. It is not about micromanaging reality. It is about alignment—resonating so deeply with a desired reality that it becomes inevitable.

But alignment cannot coexist with fear.

Spiritually, fear is an illusion—the illusion of separation, the belief that we are alone in a chaotic Universe. But when we remember that we are not just in the Universe but that the Universe is within us, fear begins to dissolve.

Surrender, then, is not about giving up. It is about giving over. It is saying:

"I trust that what is meant for me will find me. I release the how, the when, the control. I align myself with love, with faith, with certainty."

"TO MANIFEST ANYTHING INTO YOUR LIFE, YOU MUST FIRST BELIVE YOU ARE WORTHY OF RECEIVING IT."

We don't manifest from our conscious thoughts alone, but from our subconscious beliefs about what we deserve and from our self worth. Our feelings of fear and doubt are a culmination of our low self-worth, insecurities, limiting beliefs, conditioning and past experiences.

Fear and Doubt are the two things that stand in the way of Us and our dreams.

Removing fear and doubt require a commitment to inner work and to your healing journey, this is what makes manifestation such a transformative self-development practice.

When writing (WHY UNIVERSE?), the most important lesson I had to communicate about manifestation was this: we can only manifest what we subconsciously believe we are worthy of, and **the two things blocking us from having everything we desire most are FEAR and DOUBT** To attract the abundance of the universe we must begin to remove these blocks so that they no longer hold power over us. But our fears and doubts are built up over years and years, decades even, and they're not built like a tower that you can just bulldoze in one big push. Instead, it requires us to carefully, slowly, steadily remove each of the blocks one by one, in the process freeing ourselves from the weight of them.

Doubt and fear are natural emotions, but they don't have to hold you back from manifesting your desires. By understanding the root causes of doubt and fear, and implementing strategies to overcome them, you can unlock the power of unwavering faith in your manifestations.

Remember, "<u>faith is not the absence ofdoubt, but the willingness to take action despite it.</u>"

As the night deepened, the seeker rose. They gazed at the sky, the ocean, their own hands—once trembling with fear, now steady with trust.

They whispered a final message, for themselves and for you:

"Letting go is not the end. It is the beginning. The beginning of freedom, of alignment, of divine manifestation. When you release fear, you create space for miracles."

And with that, they walked forward—not into certainty of outcome, but certainty of faith.

Because when you let go of fear and doubt, the Universe finally has room to flow through you.

"I WILL ALWAYS BELIEVE THAT IF SOMEONE WANTS TO, THEY WILL, BECAUSE WHEN I WANTED TO, I DID."

-NIHAL MUDGAL

FOUR

SPIRITUAL GROWTH AND PRACTICES

⎯⎯⎯♡⎯⎯⎯

"YOUR SOUL IS THE SPARK THAT IGNITES THE FLAMES OF YOUR TRUE POTENTIAL."

Spiritual growth is a process, one that leads you inward to discover the truths that have always existed, waiting to be acknowledged. It's not a destination or a last accomplishment; rather, it's about becoming a more conscious and connected version of yourself. As you embark on this journey, you become aware of subtle shifts within, such as a gentle stirring that provides insight and serenity. You start to understand that there is something greater to life, and everything that surrounds you the individuals you encounter, the events you experience, and even the difficulties you face-is included in this grander, spiritual design.

At first, spiritual development may seem like an intangible thing, something hard to understand. But as time passes, it's evident that it's not about adhering to strict rules or chasing far-off objectives. It's about becoming one with the universe, with the true calling of your soul. It's about letting go of the small self-the version of you that is tied to ego, fear, and limitations and stepping into the higher self, the part of you that is boundless, connected to everything around you, and capable of great transformation.

As you move through life, you'll start to notice patterns, behaviors, and beliefs that have shaped your reality. Maybe you've felt stuck in certain areas of your life, unsure why things seem to repeat or why your desires don't manifest as easily as you hope. This is often a sign that there are internal blocks preventing you from aligning fully with the flow of energy around you. The key to spiritual growth lies in uncovering these blocks-limiting beliefs, fears, and past wounds and transforming them. As you become more self-aware, you begin to notice the invisible strings that hold you to particular patterns and you understand that it is possible and indeed necessary to free yourself from them.

In order to really develop spiritually, it's crucial to build *mindfulness.* This exercise of being completely present in the moment makes a huge difference on your path. Picture moving through your day, every step taken consciously, feeling every breath, and sensing the world around you in glorious detail. During these times, the din of the outside world recedes, and you can tap into your own inner reality.

Mindfulness creates the space for deeper consciousness, which makes it easier to align your energy with the universe, and thus, make manifestation happen effortlessly. When you stay present, you no longer stress about the future or rue the past. You simply exist. And in that space, the universe is free to flow through you, pushing you towards what you want with less effort.

Spiritual development, of course, does have its hurdles. One of the most potent tools on this path is **Forgiveness. We all carry around old hurts-grudges, regrets, and resentments-that keep us stuck. These energetic burdens can plug up the river of abundance and peace in our lives.** But forgiveness isn't excusing bad behavior or forgetting the past; it's releasing the emotional charge of those experiences. **"When youforgive, you free yourself from the past"**. You cease to allow it to control your destiny, and you make room for healing and transformation. It's an act of self-emancipation, a necessary part of your spiritual growth.

Another part of spiritual development is being able to **live in the present.** We tend to get caught up in the hustle and bustle of life, preparing for the future, dwelling on the past, or always pursuing the next great thing. But when we spend too much time concentrating on what's ahead or what's behind us, we're missing out on the depth of the moment.

"The universe"

doesn't exist in the past or the future-it only exists in the now.

And it's in the now that you can create your deepest desires. The more present you are, the more in sync you'll be with the flow of the universe, and the more naturally your desires will start to materialize.

Gratitude is another major aspect of spiritual development. It is simple to be caught up in thinking about what we lack or what we yet have to gain. But once you change your mindset to a place of thankfulness, you start to realize the abundance which already exists all around you. The mere process of being grateful for what you do have-your health, your loved ones, the beauty of nature-changes your energy. It allows space for more to come into your life. Gratitude is attractive. When you speak it, you resonate at the vibrational frequency of abundance, and the universe responds by bringing more of what you are grateful for.

In addition to gratitude, there are spiritual disciplines that can assist you in going deeper into the universe and assist your development.

Meditation

"The Inner Cosmos — The Sacred Art of Meditation"

The moon was low over the horizon, its silver light cast across the surface of the ocean. Gently, the waves lapped at the beach, their movement echoing the rhythm of the breath of the universe itself. Seated cross-legged on a beach rock, alone, was one figure, who looked out across the endless canvas of stars. The wind was soft, bearing the fragrance of salt and peace, and the sky was a canvas of galaxies and pearlescent stars—each one speaking in hushed tones of the universe.

This search, shrouded in stillness, did not merely look at the stars but heard from them. He had walked past deserts of uncertainty and over mountains of awareness, but today he sat and waited, looking not outwards but inwards—into the unknown world of his own consciousness. This point, so low-key and subliminal, was the birth of something intense: the opening to the eternal art of meditation.

"A Call From the Universe"

All human existence is born with a cry and a breath—a coming into a universe of noise, movement, feeling, and experience. And yet, under the cacophony of life, there is always a still, throbbing rhythm. This rhythm is the heartbeat of the world. Meditation is not a means of avoiding life; it's a way of listening for this deeper rhythm that binds all living things together.

The first time we really meditate is not always when we sit cross-legged with closed eyes on a cushion. It is sometimes when silence knocks us over—when nature quiets our busy mind, or when pain takes us to the brink that all we can do is breathe and exist. The universe tends to whisper before it roars. _Meditation is the tongue of that whisper._

Why Meditation? The Cosmic Purpose

Meditation is not a new-age invention or a trend on social media; it is an ancient spiritual tool, discovered and practiced by sages, mystics, yogis, and healers for thousands of years. Whether it was the Himalayas, the Egyptian deserts, or the forests of South America, wise beings from all parts of the Earth came to the same realization: the universe speaks in stillness.

But why should you meditate?

Because your mind is not simply a repository of memory or a thinking engine. It is an entrance—a doorway through which your consciousness may pass back and forth between levels of awareness, healing, and creation. Meditation prepares this mind to serve your soul, not as its master.

"Meditation and Spirituality: Encountering the Divine Within"

At its essence, meditation is a spiritual discipline. It is becoming home to your soul. It is being in the presence of yourself so fully that you become acquainted with the divine within. For centuries sages have claimed, **"God is not without, but within." Meditation is the key which unlocks the portal to that internal temple.**

When you sit in silence and go inward, you're not withdrawing from the world; you're entering the sacred space from where the world itself is created. In this silence, you encounter your higher self—the part of you that knows, heals, forgives, and creates. You are not just a body or a mind; you are the universe experiencing itself through your consciousness. Meditation reminds you of that sacred truth.

The Science of Stillness: What is Going On in the Brain

Where spirituality writes about soul and consciousness, science writes about neurons, frequencies, and chemistry. Thankfully, they both say the same thing but in different languages.

When you meditate:

Your brain waves relax. You move out of high-beta stress and overthinking frequencies into alpha (relaxed awareness) or theta (deep meditation and intuition) states. These states are correlated with creativity, emotional healing, and spiritual awakenings.

Your prefrontal cortex becomes activated. This is the center of consciousness, decision-making, and higher-level thinking. Consistent meditation actually remodels your brain structure to have you become a more compassionate, focused, and emotionally balanced individual.

Stress hormones reduce. Cortisol falls, heart rate returns to normal, and your immune system gets a boost. **Meditation isn't healthy for the soul alone; it's medicine for the body.**

Actually, neuroscientists have now charted what monks and mystics have long known: the brain produces adaptable. It can be reshaped. And meditation is one of the strongest weapons for positive neurological change.

The Seeker's Journey: A Story Within a Story

Let me introduce you to Rajasi, a young woman weighed down by anxiety and uncertainty. Her heart was full of questions she couldn't put into words. Despite having a caring family, a secure job, and a good life, there was an aching hollowness within her. It was as if her soul had lost a song it once sang.

One evening, unable to sleep, she strolled to the rooftop of her apartment building. The sky was uncommonly clear. The stars were shining like they had something to say. A peace started to emerge in her, even with the turmoil within. She sat down, closed her eyes, and for the first time, she didn't make her thoughts vanish. She just observed them. She breathed. She let go. That was her first meditation.

With time, Rajasi turned into a different person. She didn't transform because she meditated. She meditated and, in meditation, remembered who she really was. Her inner light, suppressed by years of conditioning and self-doubt, started to shine. And the world around her reacted. **That's the real magic of meditation—it doesn't alter you. It alters reality.**

"Techniques of Meditation: Various Paths, One Truth"

There is no single correct way to meditate. The technique is less important than the motivation behind it. The following are some eternal techniques that seekers throughout the ages have applied:

1. Breath Awareness

This is the most basic one. Just sit, close your eyes, and pay attention to your breath. Notice the cool air that goes in through your nostrils. Notice the air that goes out. This anchors your mind in the here and now.

2. Mantra Meditation

Repeating sacred sounds such as "Om," "So Hum," or personalized mantras changes your vibration. Mantras are keys that open the deeper levels of consciousness.

3. Guided Visualization

Picture yourself in a sacred forest, greeting your higher self, or bathing in cosmic light. The mind is highly receptive to imagery.

4. Loving-Kindness

Practice sending love to yourself, your loved ones, strangers, even those you dislike. This practice rewires the heart.

5. Transcendental Meditation

By the use of a secret mantra provided by an experienced instructor, this method assists you to move beyond thought itself and into pure consciousness.

"Beginner Steps: Starting Your Meditation Practice"

1. Select a quiet room. No distractions. Make it sacred—put in a candle, incense, or soothing music.

2. Sit comfortably. Don't worry about the lotus position. Use a cushion or chair if necessary.

3. Close your eyes softly. Not clenched. Allow your eyelids to rest naturally.

4. Begin with 5–10 minutes. Gradually add time as you become more comfortable.

5. Attend to the breath or a mantra. When thoughts pop up (and they will), kindly return your attention.

6. Consistency is key. Meditation benefits most from daily use. Even 10 minutes per day builds change.

7. Journal afterwards. Record how you feel, what arose, or any insight.

"The Gifts of Meditation: More Than Peace"

Self-awareness: You become aware of your emotions instead of being controlled by them.

Creativity: Meditation opens up intuitive insights and inner knowing.

Healing: Wounds in the emotional body rise to the surface and melt away in the light of your awareness.

Synchronicities: As you harmonize with the universe, magical coincidences multiply.

Manifestation: A peaceful, concentrated mind is an effective magnet for desires.

"Going Deeper: Meditation and the Laws of the Universe"

Each spiritual principle—law of attraction, vibration, cause and effect—is triggered more intensely when the mind is at peace. A chattering, distracted mind can't materialize well. But a calm, grounded one? It becomes a co-creator of the universe.

In deep meditation, you find you are not thinking your thoughts; you are observing them. And if you can observe your thoughts, you can select new ones. And if you can select your thoughts, you can recreate your reality.

Meditation is not passive. It's the most active creation tool you have.

"The Ultimate Truth: You Are the Universe Meditating on Itself"

When the seeker standing by the seaside opened his eyes, he could no longer find himself apart from the stars. He understood something eternal: what he was experiencing in meditation wasn't him viewing the universe but the universe reminding itself of something through him.

This is the secret all great beings come to learn: **Meditation is not about becoming something. It's about remembering who you already are—a soul crafted from**

stardust and spirit, a child of the divine, a shard of infinity bound in human flesh.

To Be Continued...

This meditation journey has no endpoint. There are more profound layers of quiet, more profound insights to be had, and larger expanses of consciousness to experience. But the initial step is always the same: sit, breathe, and let it be.

Throughout the chapters that follow, you will learn more about how to align with the universe. **But keep this in mind: no technique, no law, no affirmation will ever take the place of the power of stillness.**

The universe does not exist in noise. It exists in the holy silence between your breaths

Visualization

is another strong method that can speed up your spiritual development. **By vividly picturing the life you want, you give the universe a clear message of what you wish to attract.** Visualization, however, is not merely about seeing material possessions; it's about visualizing yourself living in harmony with your real purpose, experiencing the feelings of success, love, and happiness. As you do this, you align your inner energy with your outer desire, **Manifestation is a natural byproduct of your spiritual growth.**

Energy healing practices

like **Reiki, crystal therapy, or sound healing,** can assist in your process. These allow to remove blockages that make free energy exchange within your body, mind, and spirit impossible. With a balance of energy within you, it becomes simpler for you to feel your connection with your higher self and the universe, and more receptive you feel to claiming what is rightfully yours.

Finally,

"Journaling"

is a highly effective tool for introspection and spiritual development. **Recording your thoughts, feelings, and experiences has the ability to bring clarity to your path and assist you in monitoring your progress. By recording your thoughts, you provide yourself with room to process feelings, reflect on insight, and connect with your inner guidance.** Journaling assists you in looking at how far you have traveled and grounds you in your mission.

Spiritual growth and manifestation are closely connected. As you spiritually grow, you realize that manifestation is not about imposing your will on the universe; it's about being in harmony with the natural course of life. When you are in harmony your higher self and the best universe, manifestation is automatic. The more you develop your spiritual practices-mindfulness, forgiveness, gratitude, meditation-the more effortlessly your desires will manifest.

The path to spiritual growth is one of ever-expansion. It asks patience, trust, and an open heart to yield to the process. Yet, with each step that you make, you align yourself closer and closer with your own truth and the big, vast universe of possibilities. And as you settle into this more elevated reality, **you find that you begin to witness the miracles of manifestation unfold in all the various ways that it exists within your life.**

That dream was planted in your heart for a reason.

Manifest it. *-NIHAL MUDGAL*

FIVE

APPLYING UNIVERSE LAWS

The evening was still, a boundless expanse of blackness dotted with stars that twinkled like shards of celestial knowledge. Whispers on the wind were carried from out of sight, things known only to those who would listen. I sat under this endless sky with a realization settling upon me one that had required years of seeking, questioning, and gaining knowledge to realize. The universe's laws were not theories; they were the immovable pillars on which everything rested. And the secret to change was not only that one knew them but exercised them with complete conviction.

For centuries, mystics, scientists, and thinkers have attempted to decipher the workings of the universe. They have tried to grasp its rhythm, its language, and its laws. Some discovered the solutions in spirituality, others in physics, and many in self-experience, Yet, deep down, all these views merged into a single truth: The universe functions on exact, immoveable principles, and when we harmonize with them, we unleash the potential to mould our world.

"The Invisible Blueprint"

Suppose for a moment that the universe is a great river, flowing endlessly, strong yet peaceful, You are not outside of it; you are in the current. When you fight, struggle, or resist it, you feel turmoil. But when you let go, when you flow with its rhythm, life happens with breathtaking ease. This is the key to using universal laws-not controlling the flow but going with it,

From the law of attraction to the law of vibration, these doctrines underlie all the experiences that we have. They are the invisible designers behind our reality, determining everything from the kinds of relationships that we build to the possibilities that we meet. But despite their pervasiveness, so many are not even aware of how they work, mired in struggles, not knowing that the secret to transformation has always been at hand.

"The Law of Mentalism: Ideas as the Blueprints for Reality"

All beginnings start in the mind. According to the Law of Mentalism, our minds build the blueprint of our existence. Every invention, every innovation, every revolution throughout history was once an idea. The chair you sit in, the phone you're holding, the skyscrapers you see all around you those were first ideas in somebody's mind before they were concrete reality.

But here's where most people fail: they let their minds be controlled by doubt, fear, and limitation. They consider what they don't want, rather than what they do want. They concentrate on the problems, rather than the solutions. And in doing so, they unwittingly perpetuate the very situation that they think they're trying to get away from.

The universe doesn't care about good wishes; the universe cares about clarity and definiteness. As your mind gets disciplined, when your thinking turns in the direction of what you want, as opposed to the direction of your fears, life starts to happen for you. **You're not just a visitor in this world; you are a creator and you are crafting your reality by every thought you think.**

"The Law of Correspondence: As Within, So Without"

Have you ever reallized that when you're in turmoil within, the world around you seems to mirror that chaos? Relationships get strained, roadblocks pop up everywhere, and everything seems like a struggle. On the other hand, when you're at peace when you're working from a place of certainty and happiness, life moves smoothly.

This is the Law of Correspondence in action. **This law informs us that the outside world reflects the insidestate.** The universe rewards and punishes nothing; it merely reflects. If you would like to shift what you're experiencing, first shift what you believe, what you feel, and what you expect.

"The Law of Vibration: Energy in Motion"

All that exists in the universe, from the smallest atom to the largest galaxy, vibrates. Nothing is really stationary. That Implies that all emotions, all thoughts, and all intentions have their own frequency, Love, joy, and gratitude vibrate at higher frequencies than fear, anger, and doubt.

When we increase our vibration through positive feeling, through thr mindful choice, through belief in the unseen-we resonate with experiences that are similar in frequency. This is why individuals who emanate confidence draw opportunity, why those who cultivate gratitude are given more to be grateful for, and why those who live in negativity appear stuck in a never-ending loop of struggle. Knowing this law enables us to change our reality, not through force, but through frequency. It shows us that we do not have to pursue what we want; we must become the energy that naturally draws it to us,

"The Law of Attraction: The Universe's Echo"

One of the most commonly spoken about yet commonly misunderstood laws, the Law of Attraction has nothing to do with wishing something into being. It is being in alignment with that which you desire. **Youattract what you are, not what you simply want.**

Imagine that you are a tuning fork, vibrating at a certain frequency. The universe, as a giant cosmic amplifier, responds by presenting you with experiences that resonate with that vibration. If you're living in lack, you get more lack. If you're emitting abundance, abundance comes to you. It's not magic; it's resonance.

That is why it is the most successful individuals in the world because they seem to "effortlessly" draw opportunity to them. It is not chance-it is synergy. They are aligned internally with their external world.

"The Law of Cause and Effect: The Unbreakable Chain"

Every action, every decision, every choice creates ripples in the universe. **The Law of Cause and Effect teaches us that nothing occurs accidentally. There are no coincidences only effects of actions omitted or engaged in.**

This is an empowering as well as a humbling law. It indicates that we are where we are due to our circumstances, and maybe we're even aware of them. But it also means that we can transform them. Every new decision sets a new cause in action, creating a new effect. By making our decisions consciously, we can reshape our fate.

"Living in Alignment: Bringing Universal Laws into Your Everyday Life"

Universal laws are not a matter of memorizing spiritual concepts or following rituals. They are a matter of living these truths in day-to-day life.

When you awaken, intention-set. What kind of energy do you desire to carry throughout the day? What frequency do you want to radiate?

Watch your thoughts. Are they consistent with what you want or with what you fear?

Pay attention to your emotions. Are they raising your vibration or are they bringing it down?

Take inspired action. The universe does not only respond to thoughts but to action, Align your actions with your intentions.

Practice gratitude, It immediately lifts your vibration and changes your perspective from lack to abundance,

Trust the process. The laws operate whether you perceive instant results or not. Faith is the bridge between the unseen and the manifested.

The Final Truth...

As I sat under the expansive sky, reflecting on all that I had learned, I came to understand something deep: The universe is not outside of us, It is not a far-off power that gives or takes away. It is an extension of our own self, reacting to our energy, our beliefs, and our alignment.

The biggest secret is not even in leaming these laws but in understanding that they've been working all along. Our job Isn't to make them work but to realize that they already do. As soon as we release our resistance and begin aligning, the universe no longer appears to be an unpredictable energy field but rather becomes a loyal mirror reflection of our very deepest truths,

Upon this epiphany, I experienced profound peace. The pursuit was never about dominating the universe it was about recognizing that we are the universe. And when we live by its principles, life changes not through strife, but through flow.

With a heart full of thanks and a mind lit up with understanding, seeker rose to his feet, prepared to step ahead-not as a person lost seeking universal mysteries, but as a person who had finally remembered them.

"One day the tables turn. You Wake up to a life so fulfilling it feels like the Universe is thanking you for **not giving up**." *-NIHAL MUDGAL*

SIX

RISE ABOVE CHALLENGES FROM THE UNIVERSE

"The aim is to create a life you don't want to run away from. Where tranquility isn't something you pursue, but something you live day by day." – Nihal Mudgal

The moment you decide to transform your life and align yourself with the universe, something curious often happens. Challenges arise, obstacles appear, and life seems to test your resolve. You might wonder, **Why is this happening now? I'm doing everything right—why does it feel harder than before?** These are what I call the tests from the universe, and while they may feel discouraging, they are essential steps on your journey to growth and manifestation.

Imagine the universe as a wise teacher, one who doesn't hand you the answers but guides you through experiences that prepare you for the next level.*These tests are not punishments; they are opportunities to refine your intentions, strengthen your faith, and prove your readiness for the blessings you seek.*

The Seeker sat under an enormous sky full of stars, a thousand winking lights twinkling overhead like old guardians. Their heart felt heavy—not sorrowful, but questioning. They had walked the manifestation path, aligning desires with the Universe's power, being in daily gratitude, meditating daily, and imagining a life of meaning, wealth, and peace. And **still, life had suddenly started to feel. denser.**

Every time they took a step forward, it seemed like an invisible force pushed them two steps back. Unexpected bills, relationships tested, old fears resurfacing like ghosts they thought were long buried—each day carried a new trial. And so, the Seeker whispered to the stars, **"Why is this happening now?** I've been doing everything right. **Why does it feel harder than before?"**

The Universe didn't reply with lightning or flames. Rather, it replied in the subtle unfolding of experiences—the experiences that form us in silence, shaping us into something more.

And the Seeker embarked on their next journey—not a journey of manifestation, but one of mastery. A journey into the core of challenges—those divine storms rained not to shatter, but to stir us awake.

The Universe, the Wise Teacher

Envision the Universe as a teacher in every sense. It doesn't give you the answers. It doesn't yell at you. **Rather, it puts the lesson on your path**. It conceals wisdom within your pain, strength within your struggle, and light within your darkest nights.

The Seeker came to realize that **change was not always met in comfort and simplicity.** That at times, the highest harmony is achieved through challenge. The Universe, with its boundless wisdom, employs adversity not as a punishment—but as a preparation.

Every trial is a spiritual checkpoint. **A universal mirror which poses the question: "Are you prepared for what you've requested?"**

The Nature of Universal Tests

One morning, on a chilly day, the Seeker spotted a butterfly in distress trying to break free of its cocoon. Their inclination was to intervene, to softly rip open the chrysalis and set the butterfly free. But then an old sage who had watched said, **"If you help it now, it will never fly."**

Difficulties, the sage taught, are an integral part of the becoming.

And so it is with the Universe. Not every test is a wall but a womb. Not a punishment but a preparation. Before you rise, you must be reshaped. Before you lead, you must be emptied. Before you receive, you must release.

The Seeker began to understand delays as providential timing, rejection as steering, and turmoil as a stimulus. They began to see that each agonizing detour bore within it the seed of the next transformation.

Acknowledging the Patterns

Again and again, the Seeker saw a pattern. Each time they attempted to create financial independence, some unbudgeted cost would surface. Each time they imagined love, heartbreak arose. So they started to record, keeping this happening as much as randomness, but instead as messages.

Patterns set in—learnings the Universe was repeating over and over again.

"If the same test comes around again," wrote the Seeker late one evening, **"it's not because I've failed. It's because the lesson isn't done."**

The Seeker knew the Universe was exact. **It gives you exactly what youneed to grow—what you wish for, not, but what your soul is prepared to learn.** Every recurring pattern was a trail of breadcrumbs that led back to old hurts, unconscious assumptions, and unresolved emotions.

Trusting the Process

There were times when the Seeker wanted to quit. Days when their heart wailed louder than their belief. On those days, believing in the process seemed impossible.

But gradually, they started looking at life through the eyes of a higher intelligence. They remembered past moments—chances they once wept over losing, only to realize later that they were blessings in disguise. That business failure resulted in finding their real calling. That heartbreak led to opening the door to self-love.

The Seeker jotted down a mantra:
"The Universe sees the bigger picture. I only see the frame."

The Role of Resilience

Tests aren't meant to be simple. They're meant to show you to yourself.

Resilience, the Seeker came to understand, wasn't about putting on a smile and pretending all was well. It was about being tall in the storm, dripping wet, and still opting to believe in the sun.

It meant respecting their feelings—sobbing when necessary, yelling into pillows, writing through the pain—but never losing hope. Resilience was going back to their "why" time and time again.

"Why do I want this?" they would ask.

To heal. To inspire. To end cycles. To live fully.

That why became their anchor.

The Power of Perspective

There was a day when all fell apart simultaneously. The Seeker lost a contract, a friend betrayed them, and a long-sought-after goal suddenly seemed beyond their grasp. But rather than self-destruct, they stopped.

"What is this teaching me?" they asked.

And with one question, the Universe uncovered its secret curriculum.

The Seeker viewed their life as a mountain. The top from the bottom seemed impossible. But with every step up, the panorama opened. And so did they.

Every obstacle, from a higher perspective, was no longer an adversary—but a guide.

Aligning with Faith

Faith was no longer just a word. It was a frequency the Seeker decided to become.

Not blind hope, but God-trust. Trust meant deciding to have faith in the unseen. Deciding to be grateful when life didn't seem fair. Taking steps of faith while letting go of the result.

The Seeker started a practice of nightly gratitude—listing three things they were grateful for, no matter how tiny. Even on their crummiest days, they could find something: the air in their lungs, the smile of a passerby, the heat of their tea.

Appreciation opened the floodgates of trust.

The Alchemy of Surrender

One night, weary from attempting to manage everything, the Seeker strolled to the water's edge of a still lake and spoke softly into the breeze:
"I surrender."

Not in defeat, but as a statement of trust. They surrendered timelines, expectations, and the fantasy of control.

That night, a subtle change occurred.

The more they let go, the more things fell into place. Opportunities began to flow. Healing became more profound. Miracles, initially forced, were now common.

The Universe was waiting for surrender—not of dreams, but of resistance.

Embracing the Unknown

The Seeker learned to dance with the unknown. To respect uncertainty not as a threat, but as a teacher.

They started waking up thrilled by the mystery. They stopped requiring all the answers and began asking better questions:

What is this attempting to reveal to me? ,How can I evolve from this? ,Who am I becoming as a result of this? ,The more questions they asked, the more the Universe answered with precision.

Receiving the Gifts of Challenge

Reflecting, the Seeker realized that each trial had granted them something:

The heartbreak provided them with self-love.
The rejection provided them with redirection.
The waiting provided them with wisdom.
The loss provided them with presence.

They began to bless their challenges. To thank the Universe not just for the blessings, but for the breakdowns that birthed them.

Moving Forward

One day, a new soul came to the Seeker, weary and filled with doubt. "I've tried everything," they said. **"Why does it keep getting harder?"**

The Seeker smiled gently and replied,
"Because you're not being punished. You're being prepared."

They shared the story of their own journey—the fears they walked through, the nights they wept, the days they came very close to abandoning all hope.

And then they said:

"You are not alone. The Universe is your companion, not your adversary. Trust its timing, trust your becoming, and above all—trust yourself."

To everyone trekking through a storm, listen to this:

You are not broken. You are breaking open.

You are not being punished. You are being cleansed.

You are not lost. You are being led.

The Universe never presents a test without intention. **Every challenge is an invitation. To grow. To heal. To awaken. To recall who you are in your essence.**

So grow, dear Seeker—not in rebellion, but in reverence. **<u>Grow above the tests from the Universe. And become what you were meant to become.</u>**

"God lives in you. Instead of seeking Him in the distance, seek Him near & very much within you."

- Lahiri Mahasaya

SEVEN

UNVEILING THE MYSTERY OF UNIVERSE

The wind persisted that evening, as if the universe itself was waiting with bated breath. The Seeker alone stood on the hill at the back of the village, looking up at the canopy of stars spread across the dark sky. Every star glimmered like a secret, a quiet call summoning something deep inside. They had taken this nightly journey many times before, but tonight was different. There was a queer throb in the atmosphere—a beat older than time itself—that seemed to summon the soul to pay attention.

As the Seeker stood there, an idea woke up within: **What is the universe actually hiding?** Why does it sound so mysterious, yet so like home?

It had nothing to do with physics or astronomy. It had nothing to do with religion. It was something more profound—a deep understanding that the secret of the universe was not external, but internal. Something they were.

That evening set in motion a quest—not over continents, but through dimensions of awareness, inquiry, and cosmic relationship.

The Universe Within: Echoes of Stardust

Did you ever find yourself gazing up at the stars, feeling, in the very center of your soul, that they were gazing back at you?

That's how the Seeker stood, gazing upwards. Thoughts wandered back into the past, when they first heard that the atoms that make up the human body were created in the core of dying stars. That scientific fact had hit them not as a cold reality, but as a hallowed revelation.

A teacher's words rang in my mind: **"We are literally made of stardust."** But only now did the Seeker realize what it really meant. It was not just metaphorical—it was deeply true. They were the universe, considering itself.

Picture yourself a droplet of water in an ocean that is boundless, the Seeker considered. Although the drop is isolable, it is nonetheless part of the larger whole—molded by its currents, its tides, its depths. And so they were, a droplet in the boundless ocean of cosmic knowing.

The epiphany was not cognitive. It was spiritual, emotional, and passionately felt. With each breath drawn, the Seeker felt the universe breathe with them.

The Role of Curiosity: The Sacred Fire

Curiosity had long been the Seeker's north star. It smoldered deep inside, a holy flame that could not be put out by the ordinary. It was not the curiosity that drove a person to facts, but one that drove them to meaning.

As a child, the Seeker wondered at everything—not to question, but to know. Why stars shine? What is time? Where do we go when we die? These were not answers to be sought—they were invitations. Doorways into the vast unknown.

One day, they inquired of an elder, "Why do we age?"

The elder smiled. "Because time wishes to share a story—and each wrinkle is a word in that story.

That response never departed from the Seeker. It instructed them that questions are not barriers to be broken, but bridges to be crossed. It instructed that the quest was holy.

The Seeker understood that the universe is not a book to be read, but a poem to be sensed. And only those who keep asking can hear its secret rhymes.

The Language of the Universe: Signs, Symbols, and Silence

The universe does not communicate in words—it communicates in whispers. It communicates in synchronicities, in unexpected flashes of insight, in the silence that comes after a question has been asked in genuine longing.

One night, while the Seeker was meditating, they voiced out loud, "What should I do with my life?" And in that instant, a feather drifted down from a tree branch overhead and settled on their lap. There was no rational explanation, but deep within, they knew—it was a sign. Not a literal response, but an energetic one. A note from the universe.

The Seeker started seeing patterns—numbers repeating on clocks, animals appearing out of nowhere, memories of the past surfacing at exact moments. It wasn't chance. It was a language.

To decipher this code, the Seeker learned to be quiet. They meditated. Spent time outdoors. Developed awareness.

And gradually, the whispers became more distinct.

Have you ever gotten the sense that a specific song was being played especially for you? Or opened a book to a random page and read exactly what you were meant to read? That is the language of the universe in action.

It is subtle, symbolic, and highly personal.

The Dance of Science and Spirituality: Meeting in the Mystery

The Seeker used to think that science and faith were two distinct roads—one rational, one mystical. But the journey had other lessons to teach.

They learned about quantum physics: the way particles exist in many states at once until they're observed. How observation itself brings possibility crashing into reality. Isn't that what manifestation is? they asked themselves. Isn't that what prayer is?

They delved into neuroscience and found out how ideas create neural pathways, how belief reprograms the brain. They found out that the heart releases an electromagnetic field greater than that of the brain—and that emotion changes this field.

They studied epigenetics—how trauma and healing are inherited through generations—not only spiritually, but biologically.

It all started making sense.

Science was finally catching up with what wise ones had always understood: that consciousness is not in the body—the body is in consciousness. That the observer is not passive but co-creative.

And as science and spirituality danced, the mystery deepened—not in confusion, but in awe.

The Fractal of Life: As Above, So Below

The Seeker became aware of patterns everywhere—in leaves, rivers, galaxies, and emotions. Everything was repeating on different scales, as if a divine code written across reality.

They discovered fractals—mathematical designs that repeat ad infinitum. **The leaf veins reflected the tree branches, which reflected the rivers of the planet, which reflected the brain neural networks, which reflected the cosmic web of galaxies.**

It was all one.

As above, so below. As within, so without.

The Seeker perceived that the same mind that made stars blow up and re-form was the same mind mending their emotional hurts, crafting their experiences, directing their way.

It all became apparent: the universe wasn't independent of their individual journey. Their hurt, their joy, their love, and loss were all reverberations of something holy unfolding in human form.

The Illusion of Separation: Remembering the Whole

The Seeker used to think in terms of separation—that they were alone, isolated, one individual trying to make it on their own.

But the more they dug in, the more that illusion began to break down.

One day, as they sat along a river, they saw the current sweep leaves away downstream. One leaf hit against a rock and twirled out of control, another drifted serenely in the middle.

They came to understand—each leaf was responding to the same current in its own unique manner.

Just like people.

Some suffer, some surrender, some resist, and some flow. But the river remains. And all are being carried, always.

The Seeker saw that life wasn't personal. It was universal. Everything is connected. Everyone is part of the same dance, the same current, the same breath of the cosmos.

The feeling of isolation dissolved, replaced by a deep, unwavering sense of belonging—not to society, not to a tribe, but to existence itself.

From Seeking to Becoming: The Inner Return

There was a moment when the Seeker ceased seeking answers in books, in gurus, in teachings. Not because he had become disillusioned, but because something had changed.

They became the very answer they were seeking.

Their breath was sacred. Their silence was prayer. Their heart was the compass. And life itself—the mundane, the chaotic, the ordinary—was the temple.

The Seeker knew now: you don't discover the universe. You become it. You live it. You embody it.

It is in your tears, in your laughter, in your healing, in your creation. It speaks through your intuition, moves through your dreams, whispers through your instincts.

The mystery is not elsewhere. It is you.

The Closing Vision: The Universe Looking Back

On the last evening of that changing season, the Seeker stood at the same hillcrest where their questions had started. But this time, they did not ask.

They just listened.

The stars in the sky twinkled with the same light, but the Seeker's eyes perceived differently now. They no longer felt like a tiny human beneath a humbling sky—they felt like the sky itself.

A voice, not heard but impossible to deny, arose from within:

"You are not lost. You are the path.

You are not broken. You are becoming.

You are not separate. You are sacred.

You are not seeking. You are remembering."

And in that last moment, **the Seeker smiled. They had not uncovered the mystery of the universe, The mystery had uncovered them.**

The universe is not a riddle to be solved; it is a story to be experienced. And as you step into this story, you become both its author and its protagonist, co-creating a narrative that is uniquely your own.

So stand beneath the stars, breathe in their light, and remember: you are a part of the mystery, and the mystery is a part of you.

"It is not hapiness that brings us gratitude; it is gratitude that brings us hapiness".

-NIHAL MUDGAL

EIGHT

TRUST THE UNIVERSE

The night had settled over the world like a cosmic embrace, its silence carrying an unspoken wisdom. The sky stretched infinitely, a canvas of celestial wonders—distant galaxies twinkling like whispers of fate, stars shimmering with the dreams of countless souls. The moonlight kissed the surface of the ocean, casting silver ripples across the dark waters, reflecting the seeker's thoughts back to them.

As the seeker sat on the shoreline, listening to the rhythmic lull of the waves, they felt a familiar whisper—not a sound, but a knowing. It wasn't the wind, nor the distant cry of a bird; it was the Universe itself, speaking through silence, through the fabric of existence, guiding them gently yet firmly.

They had walked the path of manifestation, learned the science of intention, and seen the evidence of how thoughts shape reality. They had witnessed how belief rewires the mind, how energy interacts with the quantum field, and how the Universe responds like a mirror, reflecting the vibrations we send out.

But tonight, a deeper truth was unfolding—one that no technique or affirmation could bypass.

The Art of Trusting the Universe

Trust. Not just in the process, but in the very fabric of existence. **Trusting that what is meant for you will find you, and that the delays, rejections, and redirections are not punishments, but divine orchestrations leading you toward something greater.**

The seeker had spent years chasing certainty—trying to control outcomes, fearing the unknown. But manifestation isn't about control; it's about alignment. It is not about demanding from the Universe, but dancing with it, surrendering to the rhythm of divine timing.

Doubt crept in. "How do I know the Universe will provide? What if I'm waiting for something that will never come?"

The waves responded with their endless ebb and flow, as if whispering:

"You do not question whether the tide will return, do you? It simply does. **Trust is not about seeing—it is about knowing.**"

The Spiritual Truth of Surrender

In the depths of stillness, the seeker realized: "**Control is an illusion**". The more we grasp at certainty, the more it eludes us. True power lies not in forcing outcomes but in allowing them to unfold.

The ancient sages knew this truth:

The Taoists called it Wu Wei—effortless flow with the Universe.

<u>The Buddhists spoke of impermanence</u>—the wisdom of detachment.

<u>The mystics taught surrender</u>—trusting that the divine plan is greater than our limited vision.

To surrender is not to give up, but to give over—to release the need to dictate every step and instead embrace the unfolding journey. It is to say:

"I trust that what is meant for me will come in its own time, in its own way. I release the need to control. I align myself with love, with faith, with divine certainty."

This is not passive waiting; it is active alignment. It is embodying the energy of what we seek so fully that it becomes inevitable.

Quantum Physics and the Power of Faith

Science, too, whispers the same truth. **"The quantum world operates on probabilities, not certainties."** The observer effect in quantum physics states that the very act of observation influences reality. Particles exist in multiple states until they are observed, collapsing into a single outcome.

This is what faith does—it collapses infinite possibilities into one reality.

The quantum field does not respond to hope; it responds to certainty. If you embody the belief that your manifestation is already yours, the Universe rearranges itself accordingly. But if you doubt, the signal becomes scattered, and reality remains uncertain.

Trusting the Universe, then, is not just spiritual—it is scientific.

Healing Through Trust

The seeker sat in stillness, confronting the fears that had long held them captive:
The fear of failure.
The fear of being judged.
The fear of not being good enough.
The fear of losing what they love.

"But healing is not about rejecting fear—it is about integrating it.'

It is about holding fear in your hands, acknowledging it, and saying, "I see you, but I no longer need you to guide me."

As the seeker released these fears, a lightness filled their being. They felt the shift—not in their external world, but within.

And that is where all transformation begins.

Techniques to Trust the Universe

1. Daily Surrender Practice
Each morning, set an intention: "I release control. I trust the divine timing of my life."

2. Visualization of Flow
Imagine yourself floating down a river, effortlessly carried by the current. Feel the peace of surrender.

3. Affirmations of Trust
Rewire your subconscious with powerful beliefs:
"I trust that all is unfolding for my highest good."
"I am guided, protected, and supported."
"The Universe is always working in my favor."

4. Quantum Meditation

Sit in stillness and visualize your desired reality as if it has already happened. Not as a wish, but as a memory.

5. Gratitude Ritual

Fear lives in the future; gratitude grounds you in the present. Each night, list three things you are grateful for. Feel them deeply.

"Don't worry about how it's going to happen, otherwise you'll begin to create limitations. Just be certain about what you want and the entire Universe will rearrange itself for you. Whatever the path you might be on right now, it will support you. It will provide you with the signs to get you to where you want to be."

The 13th-century poet Rumi wrote: 'The Universe is not outside you. Look inside yourself; everything that you want, you already are. Rumi may also have agreed that the only reason the Universe might not be available to you is if you're not attuned to it. The Universe already exists within you, but it's not perceivable to you if You're not vibrating high enough. However, you can bring it to light through your words, actions, emotions and beliefs.

The Universe helps us to create, or rather, to bring possibilities into our reality. It gives you signs to follow and sends you ideas to act on. It's up to you to respond.

You might decide your goal is to work for yourself at something you enjoy. Then one day you randomly think of a specific idea, like opening your own youtube channel. If you don't think much of it, you probably won't act on it; you'll probably just dismiss it as a thought. passing

In the following weeks, you might start coming across youtubers sharing their idea which you thought about. This seems coincidental, so you continue to ignore the signs and instead invest your efforts elsewhere. But by ignoring the signs, you could be missing out on everything you want. Sometimes, we ignore the signs because we think we're supposed to achieve our goals in a particular way.

I trust where they'll take me next, knowing they'll bring me closer to where I want to be.

These days, when terms like the Law of Attraction are thrown around, **people assume that your dreams willmanifest without any effort on your part**. But you must take action on the thoughts and ideas that crop up in your mind; the inspiration that the Universe sends you. They're nudges from the Universe saying,

'Go this way! Try this!'

Intention without action is just a wish. A goal only comes to life when you decide to pursue it. The Universe is always supporting you, but you must be willing to do your part in the manifestation process.

"Embrace good vibes and learn to let things flow. There is no need to force outcomes. Once you are in harmony with the Universe, what's meant to be yours will come to you."

No one in the world has always manifested every single goal they've wanted in the time they've desired. You can change outcomes through your vibe, but you must accept that things will unfold in their own time and for your highest good - which sometimes means in a way you hadn't imagined.

Once you've learned to hone your manifestation skills, you must let go of your attachment to the goal. By trying to force or control the outcome, you breed resistance by feeding fear and doubt. When your heart is in something, only good things can follow.

Now, this may rejections not always seem true. But remember that are just redirections to better things.

<u>Setbacks are pauses for thought, opportunities to alter your plans - for the better.</u> And <u>however big anyfailure may feel at the time, there's always a lesson to learn.</u> Only with faith can we recognize the value of our apparent downfalls. What we truly want often comes wrapped in different packaging.

"Learn to let go and let things flow"

As the seeker rose, they looked once more at the vast sky, the endless ocean, and their own hands—hands that once trembled with fear, now steady with faith.

[Fundamental law of competitive strategy: "If you can't win by being better, win by being different"]

-HOW UNIVERSE?

NINE

UNIVERSE SECRET REVEALED

The evening air was crisp and still as I stood beneath an infinite canopy of stars, their celestial glow flickering softly like whispers of forgotten stories. A gentle breeze rustled through the trees, carrying with it the scent of the earth, the rhythm of the cosmos, and the quiet hum of existence itself. I was alone, yet not alone. **The universe surrounded me, embraced me, lived within me.**

This journey had not just been one of seeking knowledge—it had been a pilgrimage of the soul. I had ventured through the corridors of science, philosophy, and spirituality, grasping for answers to questions that had lingered in the depths of my being. What is the universe? What is my place in it? What is the secret that ties everything together?

And now, standing under the night sky, with the vastness stretching beyond comprehension, the answer arrived—not as a thunderous revelation but as a whisper, as if the stars themselves were speaking:

"The secret of the universe is you."

At first, the simplicity of it felt almost absurd. How could something so immense, so profoundly intricate, be distilled into such an uncomplicated truth? And yet, as the words settled within me, they resonated with a power that transcended logic. The universe, in all its infinite vastness, was not a distant entity, nor a separate force. It was within me, and I was within it.

I remembered the ancient mystics who spoke of unity, of being one with the cosmos. I thought of physicists who had uncovered the same truth through a different lens—that the atoms in our bodies are remnants of stars, that the energy coursing through us is the same force that moves galaxies. Science and spirituality, so often seen as opposing forces, were merely two languages describing the same reality. Everything was connected, woven together by threads of existence that transcended time and space.

The Journey That Led Here

Every step I had taken had led me to this moment. The struggles, the losses, the triumphs—they had not been mere coincidences. They had been part of a grand design, a symphony of experiences orchestrated by the universe to bring me closer to this realization. The challenges I had faced, the pain that had at times felt unbearable, had not been punishments but lessons. Each one had been a mirror, reflecting back the parts of myself that needed healing, growth, or transformation.

The universe had always been guiding me—not through grand gestures, but through the smallest, most subtle moments. **A book that found its way into my hands at just the right time. A stranger's words that felt like they were meant only for me. A sunrise that reminded me that even after the darkest night, light returns.**

I had spent so much time searching for answers outside of myself, looking to the heavens for signs, to teachers for wisdom, to ancient texts for hidden truths. But now, I understood. The secret was never hidden. It had always been within me, waiting to be remembered.

The Power Within

I closed my eyes, feeling the rhythm of the universe align with my own heartbeat. If the universe and I were one, then the energy I carried within me had the power to shape the world around me. Every thought, every emotion, every choice was a brushstroke on the canvas of existence.

This wasn't just a poetic idea—it was a responsibility.

For so long, I had doubted myself. I had allowed fear to dictate my path, convinced that I was small, insignificant in the grand scheme of things. But even in my darkest moments, the universe had been whispering, urging me to trust. It had spoken in the form of synchronicities that felt too perfect to be random. In the stillness of the morning light. In the quiet knowing that everything was unfolding exactly as it should.

The truth was liberating. The secret wasn't about achieving perfection or unlocking some hidden door to success. It was about living in alignment with the truth that had been there all along.

The Science of Spirituality

The realization that we are one with the universe isn't just a mystical notion—it is deeply rooted in science. Quantum physics tells us that at the most fundamental level, everything is energy. The observer effect has shown us that the mere act of observation can influence reality. This means that our thoughts, our emotions, our very state of being shape the world around us.

The energy we emit—whether it is fear or love, doubt or faith—resonates with the universe and attracts experiences that match its frequency. This is why manifestation is not about wishing for things, but about embodying the vibration of what we desire. The universe does not respond to what we want—it responds to who we are.

The Responsibility of Creation

With this understanding comes immense responsibility. **If we are the universe, then we are also its creators. We have the power to create love, healing, abundance—but we also have the power to create fear, limitation, and suffering.**

This is not to say that hardship will never come, or that life will be without pain. But knowing our connection to the universe allows us to navigate these challenges with a different perspective. **Instead of seeing obstacles as barriers, we can see them as guides.** Instead of fearing change, we can embrace it as the natural flow of existence.

The Emotional Truth

As the stars twinkled above me, I felt an overwhelming sense of gratitude—not just for the answers I had found, but for the questions that had led me here. **The mystery of the universe wasn't meant to be solved; it was meant to be lived.** Every moment of joy, every pang of sorrow, every breath was a piece of the infinite puzzle.

I thought of the people I had met along the way, the souls who had touched my life in ways they might never fully understand. The ones who had lifted me when I was low, and the ones who had challenged me to become stronger. Each of them had been part of this grand, cosmic dance, helping me remember who I was.

I opened my eyes and looked at my own hands—hands that had once trembled with doubt but now felt steady with knowing.

The universe's greatest secret was not hidden in the stars or buried in ancient texts. It was in the way we live each moment. In the love we give without expectation. In the courage we show in the face of fear. *In the way we choose to see the world—not as something separate from us, but as an extension of ourselves.*

With a deep breath, I stepped forward—not into certainty of outcome, but into certainty of faith. Because once you realize you are the universe, there is nothing to fear. The unknown is no longer something to be afraid of—it is something to be embraced.

This was not the end of the journey. It was the beginning of a deeper one. To live this truth every day. To embody the knowledge that I am both the creator and the creation, the seeker and the answer.

And so, with a heart full of wonder and a spirit ready to embrace the unknown, I stepped forward into the next chapter of my life—not as someone searching for the universe, but as someone who had finally realized they are the universe.

{"THE BIGGEST ASSET IN THE WORLD IS YOUR MINDSET"}
-NIHAL MUDGAL

About The Author

NIHAL MUDGAL is an award-winning author, manifestation expert, registered mental health counselor & founder of *UNIVERSEA* currently pursuing their medical education at Index Medical College, Indore. With a profound dedication to spirituality, self-transformation, healing, and human potential, Nihal has consistently worked to unveil the deep and intricate connections between the universe. consciousness, and the mind.

Nihal Mudgal is the author of the widely acclaimed books: **"WHY UNIVERSE?","HOW UNIVERSE?"** and **"THE COMFORT LOOP"** transformational works that have guided thousands on their journey of understanding manifestation, universal laws, healing, and aligning with cosmic energy. Nihal's distinctive approach harmonizes ancient spiritual wisdom with cutting-edge psychological and scientific insights, empowering readers with practical tools to awaken their true potential.

A lifelong learner and seeker, Nihal holds a Professional Diploma in Clinical Psychology from the renowned University Emo Matrix, and is now an officially registered and practising *Mental health counselor* in India, the United States, and the United Kingdom. This allows Nihal to bring a truly global and interdisciplinary perspective to the fields of healing and mental well-being

Nihal's work continues to inspire individuals across the globe to step into their highest selves, co-create their realities with the universe, and live purposefully. Drawing inspiration from diverse philosophical and spiritual traditions, and integrating insights from neuroscience, quantum physics, psychology, and economics, Nihal helps individuals transform their lives through inner alignment and universal understanding.

Their contributions to the realm of manifestation, emotional healing, and personal evolution have been honored with ***The prestigious 2025 Influencer Book of Records Award***. Beyond writing, Nihal is deeply committed to educating and equipping people with the wisdom, clarity, and tools needed to heal, grow, and manifest a life of abundance, impact, and joy.

Message From The Author

Dear Reader,

The journey of manifestation is not just about attracting what you desire—it is about transforming yourself from within, aligning with the universe, and unlocking the limitless potential that resides within you. Through my books, I have sought to bridge the gap between science and spirituality, offering you not just theories, but practical wisdom and techniques that can truly reshape your reality.

Why Universe? was born from the curiosity to understand the universe's role in our lives, while

How Universe? emerged as a guide to applying these universal principles with precision. Each page is designed to help you navigate the unseen forces that influence your path, overcome challenges, and step into the life you are meant to live.

I truly believe that manifestation is not just a process—it is a way of life. The universe listens, responds, and guides those who are willing to trust its timing and wisdom. As you embark on this journey, I encourage you to embrace gratitude, remain open to signs, and most importantly, believe in your own power.

Thank you for allowing me to be a part of your spiritual and transformational journey. May these words serve as a guiding light, helping you manifest a life filled with abundance, joy, and purpose.

With gratitude,
NIHAL MUDGAL